HAWAI'I'S
BEAUTIFUL BIRDS

TEXT BY H. DOUGLAS PRATT

PHOTOGRAPHS BY JACK JEFFREY AND H. DOUGLAS PRATT

MUTUAL PUBLISHING

Red-Tailed Tropicbird

Common Fairy-Tern

Hawaiian Coot

The mid-ocean mountaintops that we call the Hawaiian Islands received their plants and animals as chance arrivals that could survive 2,500-mile ocean journeys from the nearest continents. The Islands' generous rainfall and balmy trade winds provided a benevolent environment for the successful few. From these chance ancestors, an array of species unique to Hawai'i gradually evolved.

• The Hawaiian Eden included no land mammals, no amphibians, nor reptiles or mosquitoes. Here, birds could safely lose the power of flight, which many did. Plants could lose their thorns and chemical defenses. And by interisland colonization, many species could evolve from a single ancestor.

• This world, which was like no other, began to change about 1,500 years ago with the arrival of humans from islands to the south. About half of Hawai'i's unique birds, including almost all of the flightless ones, became extinct between the coming of the Polynesians and the arrival of Europeans. We know these hapless birds only from their bones. Following Captain Cook's "discovery" of the

Islands, Hawaiian birds faced new challenges and many could not cope with the rapid changes. As native birds died out, island people imported replacements from around the world. In this respect, Hawai'i's birds mirror her human population with the first community now reduced to a remnant and outnumbered by recent immigrants.

• Today, nearly all of the flowers and trees seen in Waikiki are imports that can be seen in any tropical resort, and the birds can be found in cages in any pet store. But, like modern Hawai'i's people, her present-day birds form a beautiful and cosmopolitan community that is unique in its own right.

• In the following pages you will meet the surviving native birds, as well as their immigrant neighbors. We hope that these photos will pique your curiosity and make you visit some of Hawai'i's remaining wild areas. But, even if you visit only Waikiki, this book will help you to appreciate the birds that today inhabit what Mark Twain called "the loveliest fleet of islands that lie anchored in any ocean."

Library of Congress Catalog Card
Number: 96-76819
ISBN 1-56647-120-6

First Printing, October 1996
Second Printing, July 1998
Third Printing, March 2001
3 4 5 6 7 8 9

Design by Angela Wu-Ki

Mutual Publishing
1215 Center Street, Suite 210
Honolulu Hawaii 96816
Ph (808) 732-1709
Fax (808) 734-4094
Email mutual@lava.net
www.mutualpublishing.com

Printed in Taiwan

TABLE OF CONTENTS

'I'iwi with native raspberry

Photo Credits: *All photos by Jack Jeffrey, except those indicated by the initials DP, which are by Douglas Pratt. The two paintings are by Douglas Pratt.*

EVOLUTION ON ISLANDS:

The Hawaiian Honeycreepers

Scientists believe that among the first birds to colonize the Hawaiian Islands was a rather undistinguished species of finch related to such mainland birds as goldfinches, crossbills, and redpolls. This seed-eating finch founded a dynasty that became the dominant group among Hawaiian forest birds. We know them today as the Hawaiian honeycreepers, because many species feed on nectar, but in fact they exhibit a range of variation unequaled in any continental bird family. Unfortunately, many of the variants are now extinct, but enough survive to provide an exciting picture of the phenomenon scientists call *adaptive radiation.*

Representative Honeycreepers

Palila

'Akepa

'Akikiki

Hawai'i Creeper

Maui 'Alauahio

VARIATION ON A THEME

Some of the descendants of the first honeycreeper, such as the **Palila**, adapted for eating seeds of the mamane tree, retain the thick finch bill, but most have it modified in some way to adapt to new plants and new foods. The bill of the **'Akepa** looks superficially finchlike, but has crossed tips (which you can see if you look closely) used to pry apart the scales of leaf buds in the search for insects. The **'Akikiki**, also called Kaua'i Creeper, is an ersatz nuthatch that picks insects from the bark of trees, while the **Hawai'i Creeper** behaves similarly, but likes smaller branches and twigs. The **Maui 'Alauahio**, also called Maui Creeper, uses its simple straight bill much like continental warblers to glean insects from leaves and bark. On Kaua'i, the **'Anianiau** has a similar bill, but its brush-tipped tubular tongue adapts it for nectar as well as

'Anianiau

insects. Other honeycreepers, such as the abundant crimson **'Apapane** and the fancy **'Akohekohe** or Crested Honeycreeper have slightly down-curved bills and sip nectar from the shallow flowers of ohi'a-lehua. The 'akohekohe even returns the favor by distributing pollen with its bushy crest. Other nectar-feeders have strongly curved bills that fit the tubular corollas of many native flowers. They include the spectacular **'I'iwi** and the **Kaua'i 'Amakihi**, which has close relatives on the other islands.

To these varied, but rather conventional, birds we can add the rare **Maui Parrotbill**, whose huge bill and powerful neck muscles enable it to crush twigs and wrench off strips of wood and bark in its search for insect larvae. But perhaps the most bizarre of all is the Big Island's 'Akiapola'au (next page).

'Apapane

'Akohekohe

Maui Parrotbill

Kaua'i 'Amakihi

'I'iwi

'Akiapola'au male

WHATEVER WORKS:
THE AMAZING 'AKIAPOLA'AU

'Akiapola'au female

Woodpeckers are very poor at crossing salt water, and none ever reached Hawai'i. The woodpecker niche was filled, Rube Goldberg fashion, by one of the curve-billed Hawaiian honeycreepers. Holding its thin upper bill out of the way, the **'Akiapola'au**, or 'Aki' for short, uses its straight lower bill to peck at the bark (the Hawaiian name means, roughly, "hammerhead"). Then the upper one comes into play to winkle grubs out of the cracks. The bright yellow males have bigger bills and somewhat different feeding sites than the grayer females.

'Akiapola'au

Kokia • DP

'Ohe naupaka • DP

Clermontia • DP

'I'iwi

Wiliwili • DP

IT ALL FITS THE BILL

Hawaiian honeycreepers also exhibit *coevolution*, a process in which two or more organisms evolve simultaneously and develop mutually beneficial characteristics. In Hawai'i, many plants from a variety of families have developed curved tubular flowers that may differ strikingly from flowers of their relatives. Such flowers fit the bills of nectar-feeding birds like a glove on a hand and have the pistil placed so it can pick up pollen from the bird's forehead. The **'I'iwi** shown here is feeding in the curved flowers of *Stenogyne*, a native mint. The red ***Kokia*** flowers are related to hibiscus, but the petals are rolled into a curved tube. **'Ohe naupaka** is a Kaua'i mountain relative of the straight-flowered *Scaevola* bushes common on tropical beaches. In the lobelia family, ***Clermontia*** has prominent pistils that are an almost perfect fit for the 'I'iwi. Even the **wiliwili** shows much more curvature than one expects in a member of the pea family.

MODERN HAWAI'I'S AVIAN MELTING POT

Great Frigatebird • DP

If you confine your Hawai'i vacation to resort areas such as Waikiki, Ka'anapali, or Kona, you are unlikely to see a native honeycreeper. But birds are always around (even sometimes on your breakfast table!) and a little attention to them will broaden your tropical horizons. In this section we will take you on a bird tour of the Hawai'i seen by most visitors, and the only Hawai'i known to a surprisingly large number of residents, most of whom, after all, dwell in cities and towns.

Brown Booby

View of Honolulu • DP

Fairy-Tern egg • DP

Common Fairy-Tern

Young chick • DP

A Few Natives

Although Hawai'i's urban areas may look like concrete jungles, they still support a few intrepid native birds. Because the ocean is always nearby, seabirds are often a part of Hawai'i's urban landscapes. **Great Frigatebirds** seem to hang effortlessly in the air high above city streets, and sunbathers at Waikiki are familiar with **Brown Boobies** that course back and forth just offshore. Especially interesting is the **Common Fairy-Tern,** a true urban resident. Although it is a seabird that feeds on small fish, this graceful tern needs trees just as much as it needs the ocean. It has the remarkable habit of laying its single egg on a bare branch without any semblance of a nest. When the fuzzy

chicks hatch, they remain on the spot to be fed by their parents. The older chick has long claws on webbed feet which enable the youngster to cling to swaying branches even in high winds. Visitors to Kapi'olani Park in Waikiki or the grounds of the Hawai'i State Capitol can observe these delicate fliers, which the Hawaiians called *manu o Ku,* "the bird of peace," or may see the chicks and adults perched in large trees. Of course, one must be careful not to confuse them with the much heavier and less graceful white **feral pigeons,** descendants of European Rock Doves, that are also abundant in the parks.

Also conspicuous in city parks is the **Pacific Golden Plover,** one of

Hawai'i's most familiar birds. Golden plovers, or *kolea* in Hawaiian, nest in Alaska and migrate to Hawai'i for the winter months. Here, they occupy winter feeding territories in open grassy areas. The same bird will often be in the same spot day after day.

When they first arrive in the fall, they are rather drab, with dirty white underparts and brown upperparts flecked with gold, but they begin to grow black feathers on the breast as the season progresses. By spring they sport a very handsome breeding plumage. Males develop more black than females. It's fun to watch your favorite plover undergo the transformation.

Feral Pigeon • DP

Pacific Golden Plover molting • DP

Older chick

Pacific Golden Plover Fall juvenile

Pacific Golden Plover Spring male

One of the first birds the mainland visitor to Hawai'i notices is the **Common Myna**. It is common, bold, and conspicuous and hangs around airports and hotels on all the islands. It is not found in Europe or North America, but has been in Hawai'i since the mid-1800's, when it was introduced from India, supposedly to control insect pests. Mynas are entertaining birds with behavior similar to that of the European Starling, a common mainland relative. Like most starlings, mynas gather in noisy roosts at night, often in dense trees, such as mango, that grow near buildings. Parking under a myna roost can provide a rude awakening the next day! Also immediately noticeable are Hawai'i's two common doves. The little **Zebra Dove**, named for the black-and-white stripes on the sides of its breast, is so bold as to have become a pest in open-air restaurants, where they may land right on your plate! Feeding them is not a good idea for obvious reasons of sanitation. These perky doves, native to

Zebra Dove

Common Myna

Spotted Dove

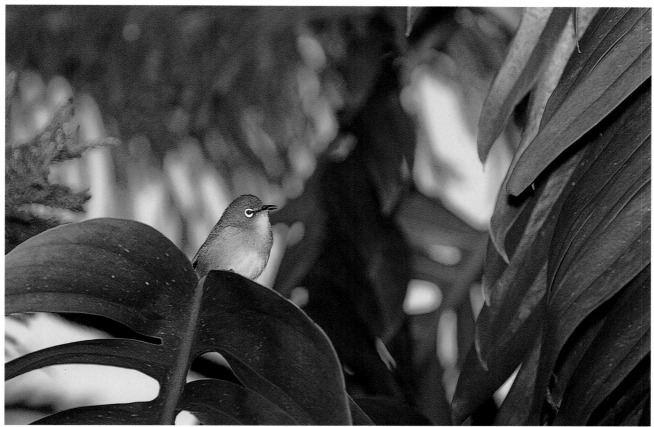

Australia, are the source of one of the most familiar sounds in Hawai'i today—the *coo-coo-coo-coo* notes with a rhythm like Morse Code. A bit more reserved, though still quite tame around hotels, is the much larger **Spotted Dove**. These plump, pink-breasted birds strut about. Like the mynas, they might well be called *kama'aina* birds. (The term refers to non-Hawaiian families who have lived in the islands for generations.) Their ancestral home is southeast Asia.

Visitors to Waikiki will certainly notice the two bulbuls, introduced in the 1960's, probably as escaped cage birds. Because both of them are crested, some people think they are related to cardinals, but they are native to India and belong to a family that has no American representatives. The **Red-whiskered Bulbul** is the smaller of

the two, with white underparts and a very spiky crest. The larger and more common **Red-vented Bulbul** is ubiquitous now on O'ahu and can even be found at the tops of the mountains in dense forest. Both bulbuls are potential threats to native forests and agriculture, particularly for growers of guava, papaya, and other soft fruits. Fortunately, bulbuls seem to hate to fly over salt water and will not spread to other islands without human assistance.

The doves, mynas, and bulbuls are hard to miss, but to identify the numerous smaller birds you will have to look a little closer. One of the most common (some say the most abundant bird in Hawai'i now) is a little green-and-yellow bird with a bold ring of white around each eye that flits about among flowers and leaves in search of

Red-whiskered Bulbul • DP

Red-vented Bulbul • DP

insects and nectar. It is the Japanese White-eye known as *mejiro* in its native Japan. Despite its size, it has an impressive tinkling song that may wake you at dawn. Be careful not to mistake the white-eye for the Yellow-fronted Canary, another small bird with a lot of yellow in its plumage. The canary, a native of southern Africa, has a seed-eating bill and sings a wonderfully melodic song not quite as complex as that of the familiar yellow canary. Yellow-fronted Canaries love the ironwood trees in Kapio'lani Park but have also spread into native forests on the Big Island. They can be seen on the ground, as well as in the treetops.

Another tiny bird likely to be seen on grassy lawns is the Java Sparrow, with bold white cheeks and a huge coral-pink bill. Java Sparrows sometimes travel in huge flocks and can be devastating to grain and other crops. Their importation into the U. S. has been prohibited for years, but they were slipped into Hawai'i anyway in the 1960's and are now spreading, unfortunately, like wildfire.

Another kama'aina bird is the House Finch, a native of North America. Female House Finches are drab, streaky-brown birds, but the males are washed with raspberry-red, yellow, or orange. The Hawaiian population has a much higher percentage of orange and yellow males than do those on the mainland. It is interesting to see how many of the odd-colored males you can find. House Finches are mainly seedeaters, but they are not very picky eaters and have adapted to a wide variety of habitats in the islands. Completing the geographic mix are several brightly colored birds from South America.

Yellow-fronted Canary

Java Sparrow

House Finch

Northern Cardinal female

Northern Cardinal male

CARDINALS AND COUSINS

Most Americans are familiar with the **Northern Cardinal**, as least as a sports mascot, but are surprised to see it in Hawai'i. Introduced in the 1930's, cardinals have done very well in the Islands. They are widespread but are never as abundant as house finches or white-eyes. In the Northern Cardinal, males and females differ in color, but in the **Red-crested Cardinal**, an import from Brazil, they are alike. (The brown-headed birds you see are juveniles.) Red-crested Cardinals are common on O'ahu, but are not as widespread on the outer islands as the Northern Cardinal. On the Big Island, a cousin of the Red-crested called the **Yellow-billed Cardinal**, also from South America, is common and conspicuous in the Kona area. It lacks the crest that distinguishes the other cardinals. Like Zebra Soves, Yellow-billed Cardinals can become very tame around restaurants and may beg for handouts at your table. Kona also is home to another immigrant from South America—the brilliant-yellow **Saffron Finch**. Look for it around the Keahole Airport and in rural areas of Kona and South Kohala.

Red-crested Cardinal

Yellow-billed Cardinal

Saffron Finch

Cattle Egret

ALONG RURAL ROADSIDES

If you leave the resort areas and drive into Hawai'i's scenic countryside, you are sure to notice birds along the roadside. Some of these will be the same as those you met in more developed areas, but others can be seen only away from town. The graceful white birds with long yellow legs and bills that you see around livestock and following mowing machines are **Cattle Egrets**. These remarkable birds evolved on the plains of Africa, where they followed grazing animals and fed on insects and other small animals stirred up by the herd. In relatively recent times, taking advantage of newly opened forests and the spread of cattle raising, the egrets spread from Africa as far as North and South America and Australia. Cattle egrets were brought to Hawai'i in the 1950's, ostensibly to control cattle pests, and they have thrived here. Those egrets living near airports, however, can

Wild Turkey • DP

be problematic for aircrafts. Whether they would have ever reached Hawai'i on their own, we will never know.

The idea of introducing birds as a food source is as old as the first Polynesian settlers. They brought with them wild fowl chickens that were little changed genetically from the wild **Red Junglefowl** of southeast Asia. These ran wild in the forests of Hawai'i and are

still common along roadways today, at least on mongoose-free Kaua'i. The cocks and hens look like small game chickens, but note that their legs are usually dark gray or reddish, rather than the golden yellow of domestic fowl. The biggest difference shows up in the downy young, which are streaked like baby pheasants, rather than yellow like barnyard chicks. With the idea of

Red Junglefowl cock • DP

Red Junglefowl hen • DP

Junglefowl chicks • DP

Black Francolin • DP

Gray Francolin • DP

Erckel's Francolin • DP

adding to Hawaiian food resources, Captain Vancouver presented King Kamehameha I with turkeys from North America. The King liberated them on the Big Island and forbade hunting them for several years so they could become established. Today, **Wild Turkeys** are frequently seen on the island's ranch lands.

Other game birds have been introduced in recent times. Particularly noticeable around resort areas are three species of francolin (say FRANC-olin, not fran-COLIN). Probably the one most familiar to casual observers is the **Gray Francolin**, commonly seen on

golf courses on Maui and the Big Island. These dusty-brown partridges with orange throats are attracted to irrigated places in the midst of a dry habitat. In the same places, look for the handsome **Black Francolin**, with its white cheeks and chestnut collar. Female black francolins could be mistaken for grays, but they have a patch of chestnut on the back of the neck. Both the gray and the black francolin come from southern Asia. The much larger **Erckel's Francolin** has a wider habitat preference and can even be found on the edge of forest along Koke'e Road on Kaua'i. It is easily identified by its

chestnut cap and longitudinally streaked breast. Erckel's Francolins are becoming increasingly scarce in their native range in the highlands of Ethiopia and Eritrea because of forest destruction, but they are thriving in Hawai'i. The **Chukar** is another introduced partridge often noticed by visitors. It inhabits dry, rocky areas in the Middle East and has adapted to similar places in Hawai'i, such as the barren summit area of Haleakala on Maui. The **Common Peafowl** was brought to the Islands more for ornament than for food. These handsome birds from India are not widespread, but have

Chukar

Common Peafowl • DP

Short-eared Owl

lived on the ranch lands of South Kohala on the Big Island for well over a century. Before the coming of cattle ranching, open habitats were rare in Hawai'i so it is not surprising that few native birds are found in such places. Two, however, have taken advantage of open fields. On all islands, look for the day-flying **Short-eared Owl**, known locally as the Pueo. It often soars over woods and fields in the manner of a hawk. Hawai'i's only true hawk is the 'io or **Hawaiian Hawk**, which is confined to the Big Island, where it hunts over cane fields, lava flows, and even the streets of Hilo, as well as mountain forests.

Hawaiian Hawk

Nutmeg Mannikin

Orange-cheeked Waxbill • DP

Common Waxbill

Warbling Silverbill

LITTLE BIRDS IN THE GRASS

Almost any pet store in the world will feature tiny finches and waxbills. These colorful and interesting pets have been popular for centuries, and many have been released in Hawai'i. In the wild they usually inhabit grassy areas where they feed on grass seeds at various stages of development. They travel about in flocks, with, sometimes, hundreds of birds. The **Nutmeg Mannikin** from southeast Asia became so numerous in 19th-century Hawai'i that it wiped out early attempts to grow rice in the islands, hence its local name, "ricebird." A more recent arrival, the African **Common Waxbill**, has become so abundant on O'ahu that, at a distance, flocks look like swarms of bees. Mannikins (not to be confused with the manakins of the American tropics) tend to be patterned in brown and black with dark bills, whereas the closely related waxbills, such as the **Orange-cheeked Waxbill** now common in parts of O'ahu and spreading on Mauai, are often brightly colored with red bills that resemble old-fashioned sealing wax. The **Warbling Silverbill**, a bird of dry African savannahs, fits neither category and has a metallic bill. It has become abundant in savannah-like parts of the Big Island and is spreading to similar habitats on Maui, Moloka'i, and O'ahu.

Japanese Bush-Warbler • DP

Sky Lark

Melodious Laughing-thrush

Singers in the Woods and Fields

Sadly, most native birds had disappeared from the areas where people lived in Hawai'i by the middle of the nineteenth century due to destruction of the habitat. Foreign birds were often introduced to replace vanished native species. Many of these were brought to the Islands more for their beautiful songs than for their plumage. In open, grassy country on the Big Island and Maui, look for sparrow-like birds with white outer tail feathers flying up from the shoulder of the road. These are **Sky Larks** that came to Hawai'i from England via New Zealand. Although not very colorful, Sky Larks have a spectacular vocal display. They circle high overhead, often nearly out of sight, pouring forth a ringing cascade of song that seems to

fill the air. It is easy to understand the poets' fascination with this drab-colored bird. Similarly, the Japanese have long held the **Japanese Bush-Warbler** in high esteem, although it is not much to look at and is so secretive that few people ever see the author of the haunting whistles that have become one of the characteristic sounds of forests on O'ahu and Maui. The bush-warbler, *uguisu* in Japanese, named in imitation of its song, is now spreading to other islands in Hawai'i. In similar forests you may also hear the loud, vigorous, and varied whistled song of the **Melodious Laughing-thrush**, a prized cage singer in China, where it is called the *hwa-mei*. It is said that these birds were introduced to Hawai'i during the Chinatown fire in Honolulu earlier this

century, when many were liberated by their owners to save them from the flames. Whatever the case, they are now common on Kaua'i, Maui, and the Big Island, as well. In the bird markets of Singapore and other southeast Asian cities, the most prized singer of all is the **White-rumped Shama**, a true thrush that is almost as lovely to look at as it is to hear. It was brought to Hawai'i over half a century ago and now fills the forests of O'ahu and Kaua'i with its lush, liquid and gurgling flutelike notes. Also popular with oriental bird keepers is the **Red-billed Leiothrix**, which used to be called the Hill Robin. It has a rolling robin-like song and has, indeed, taken to the hills in Hawai'i. It is now quite common in forests of all types from O'ahu to the Big Island.

White-rumped Shama

Red-billed Leiothrix

Wandering Tattler

AVIAN VACATIONERS ON THE SHORE

On any drive in Hawai'i one is never far from shorelines, where one can find the only group of native birds that still survive in the lowlands. Sandpipers, plovers, and their relatives nest in the arctic but "vacation" in Hawai'i during the winter months. You have already met the Pacific Golden Plover, which chooses a wide variety of habitats. Other species are more often seen along shores. The **Ruddy Turnstone** ('akekeke in Hawaiian) and the **Wandering Tattler** (*'ulili*) are two that are frequently seen. The tattler is named for its ringing call, imitated by singers of the popular Hawaiian song "Ulili e." The very pale **Sanderling**, whose Hawaiian name *huna kai* means "sea foam," will already be familiar to many visitors. Sanderlings are the little birds that retreat like wind-up toys before the waves on beaches worldwide. Hawai'i's shorebird visitors even include an endangered species, the **Bristle-thighed Curlew**. The curlew nests only in Alaska and, during the winter, scatters over the far-flung islands of the tropical Pacific. They winter regularly in the uninhabited Northwestern Hawaiian Islands, but on the main islands they are mainly spring and fall transients. They prefer open, grassy areas.

Sanderling • DP

28

Ruddy Turnstone

Bristle-thighed Curlew • DP

ENDANGERED BIRDS
OF ENDANGERED WETLANDS

For the ancient Hawaiians the staff of life was poi, made from taro root. Taro grows in water, so vast areas of the lowlands of Hawai'i were made into ponds somewhat like rice paddies. As a protein source, Hawaiians also farmed salt-water fish in artificial shoreline ponds ringed with lava rock. Both of these activities created ample habitat for a group of native wetland birds. Because shoreline land is much more valuable today for resort development, these habitats are now preserved only in a few refuges, such as **Hanalei National Wildlife Refuge** on Kaua'i. Because the habitat is endangered, so are most of the birds found there, although the birds may seem abundant at a given site. (Keep in mind that only a few such places exist, so the total population of freshwater birds is small.) Probably the most noticeable one is the **Hawaiian Stilt** because of its rather annoying yipping calls. One smart-aleck dubbed it the "pond poodle!" Actually, stilts are graceful

Left: Hanalei National Wildlife Refuge • DP

Hawaiian Stilt

Hawaiian Coot

Common Moorhen

Hawaiian Duck • DP

Black-crowned Night-Heron

Juvenile Night-Heron • DP

and handsome birds with black-and-white plumage and long, coral-pink legs. Also widespread in the Islands is the ducklike **Hawaiian Coot**. It is not a duck—notice its white chicken-like bill with a big knob on the forehead. A similar, but more colorful, bird is the **Common Moorhen**, with a red bill. Although it belongs to a common worldwide species, the Hawaiian population is endangered. The moorhen is much shier than the coot and can be seen only on Oʻahu and Kauaʻi. It lurks in shoreline vegetation and only rarely swims in open water like the coot. There is, of course, a true **Hawaiian Duck** that is related to the familiar Mallard, but it survives in genetically pure form only on Kauaʻi. Although the drakes and hens can be distinguished, both look more or less like female Mallards. One Hawaiian wetland bird that is not endangered is the **Black-crowned Night-Heron**, the same one that is found almost worldwide. It is Hawaiʻi's only resident native heron, but you might think that the streaky brown juveniles are a different species. During the last century, when wetlands were more widespread in Hawaiʻi, the islands were popular with waterfowl hunters, but too few ducks are present now to allow for sport hunting. Nevertheless, a few familiar mainland ducks and geese manage to find their way to the islands each winter. The most common is the **Northern Shoveler** with its distinctive broad bill. The **Northern Pintail** often arrives without its characteristic long central tail feathers, but grows them in by spring. Even the smaller forms of the **Canada Goose** occasionally show up and should not be confused with the native Nene (see next section).

Northern Shoveler • DP

Northern Pintail • DP

Canada Goose • DP

Nene at Kilauea Caldera • DP

Nene

'Ohelo • DP

Pukiawe

Kukaenene • DP

SAGA OF THE NENE, HAWAI'I'S STATE BIRD

One does not expect to find a goose living in nearly barren lava flow regions far from fresh water. But the Hawaiian Goose, or **Nene**, has adapted well to such unexpected habitats. Note the reduced webbing between the toes. It feeds on a variety of fruits of low shrubs that pioneer on lava flows. These include a Hawaiian huckleberry called **'ohelo**, the stiff-branched **puki-awe**, whose dry berries look like pink porcelain, and **kukaenene**, so named because its purple-black berries so often color nene droppings! Because

they evolved in the absence of terrestrial predators, the native geese had little fear of man, a characteristic that they still exhibit today. They probably survived into modern times only because they lived in the saddle between Mauna Loa and Mauna Kea, an area considered *kapu* (forbidden) and feared by the Hawaiians. Nene were saved from extinction by an active campaign of captive breeding and release of birds into protected areas. Although these efforts have restored them to national park lands

Nene • DP

Nene with admirers • DP

on Maui and the Big Island, they still do not have self-sustaining populations on those islands. Part of the reason may be that these habitats are not ideal for their goslings who do not receive proper nutrition from their food. The goslings become weak and are more vulnerable to predators like the **mongoose**. The mongoose, an alien predator introduced a century ago to control canefield rats, but which "controlled" native ground-nesting birds instead. Recently, Nene have been released on mongoose-free Kaua'i and appear to be thriving there. They can be seen easily at Kilauea Point. They usually are found in small groups—probably families. Males and females look alike, but first-year young have less contrasting colors. The dark streaks on the sides of the neck are not the result of pigmentation but actually are deep furrows in the soft feathers. Several mainland geese exhibit this same phenomenon. When Hawai'i became a state, the endearing and tame Nene, which at that time had just been brought back from the brink of extinction, became its State Bird.

Mongoose

Nene family

MOUNTAIN FORESTS:
The Natives' Last Hope

Alaka'i Wilderness, Kaua'i • DP

Why do we not see native songbirds around resort areas? In most parts of the world, even areas that have seen comparable ecological alteration retain at least some of their natural inhabitants. Hawai'i's native forest birds are absent even from seemingly good habitat at low elevation. To see them one has to venture to mountain forests above 3,000 feet. The reasons are insidious and complex, but are now fairly well understood. Hawaiian birds evolved in isolation from most bird diseases. Many of these are spread by mosquitoes so, even though migratory shorebirds and ducks might have carried such things as bird pox and avian malaria, no vectors were present to transfer them to the resident birds. The first mosquitoes came to Hawai'i in the early nineteenth century in the water casks of a ship from Central America. These tropical invaders became established in the lowlands, but did not do well in the cooler upper forests. Once the vector was present, bird diseases ravaged the natives just as European diseases decimated the Hawaiian people. Now, native forest birds cling to existence in their mountain forest refuges, but they are under constant assault.

'Apapane with mosquito

'Apapane

THE BIG TWO AND THE BIG THREE

Unlike mainland rain forests, which may have hundreds of tree species forming the forest canopy, those in Hawai'i are relatively species-poor. Where rainfall is high, as in the upper reaches of Kaua'i, the entire canopy may be of a single kind of tree, the usually red-flowered ohi'a-lehua (ohi'a for short). It is a remarkable performer ecologically, being one of the pioneer plants on lava flows as well as the dominant tree in climax forests. Although rarely straight enough to be an important timber tree, ohi'a's gnarled and twisted trunks and branches define the character of Hawaiian forests. Its brush-like flowers lack petals. Its stamens grow out of a cuplike calyx in which nectar, the main food source for the nectar-feeding honeycreepers, collects. The other important canopy tree in Hawaiian forests is **koa**. The koa's sickle-shaped leaves belie the fact that it is actually an acacia. Unlike ohi'a, koa is an important forestry tree. It usually grows mixed with ohi'a

'I'iwi

Hawai'i 'Amakihi

Koa • DP

in slightly drier areas and rarely forms a closed canopy itself. These "big two" trees support a trio of honeycreepers, with representatives on all the main islands. The locally abundant **'Apapane** is the honeycreeper most likely to be noticed by the casual observer. They are hard to miss in places like Hawaii Volcanoes National Park. They are easily identified by the bold white feathers under the tail that contrast with their crimson body feathers. Lacking the white under the tail is the scarlet **'I'iwi**, with its amazing sickle-shaped bill. It is less common than the 'Apapane, but is still easy to find in certain places on Kaua'i, Maui, and Hawai'i. Any native forest that is high enough will have both of these red birds, as well as one of the three species of 'amakihi. All three have downcurved bills shorter than that of the 'I'iwi and yellow-green plumage with a black "mask" that gives them a slightly evil, squinty look. The **Hawai'i 'Amakihi** is found from Moloka'i to the Big Island, while O'ahu and Kaua'i each have their own distinct species. (See below for the Kaua'i 'Amakihi.) At one time there was a fourth honeycreeper common to all the larger Hawaiian Islands—the **'O'u**, a chunky green bird with a yellow head and a thick hooked bill. Sadly, the 'O'u is now nearly extinct and was never photographed by serious photographers with good equipment. We can show only a rather grainy shot taken by Pratt on Kaua'i in 1975. Except for the "big three," each of the larger islands has its own collection of distinctive species.

'O'u • DP

ʻOmaʻo

THE BIG ISLAND'S RICH RAIN FORESTS

Because it is more than twice as large as all the other islands combined and is formed mostly by two of the world's tallest mountains (measured from their base on the sea floor), Hawaiʻi has a much greater range of habitats and much more mountain forest at sufficient elevation to support native birds than any of the others. These forests harbor the richest surviving native bird community in Hawaiʻi. It includes members of several other bird families, as well as the "big three" honeycreepers and others unique to the Big Island. The **Hawaiʻi ʻElepaio** belongs to a group of flycatchers found from Australia to the Pacific

Hawaiʻi ʻElepaio

42

islands. It is a friendly and confiding bird, whose namesake whistles are a characteristic sound of most forest types on Hawai‘i. Its plumage varies from place to place, depending on rainfall. This individual shows by its rich chestnut plumage that it is from a wet habitat. Another non-honeycreeper is the **‘Oma‘o**, related to thrushes and solitaires of North America. The bird is hard to see with its dull gray and brown plumage, but its lively song is hard to miss and is unlike that of any other Hawaiian bird. The song is easy to hear around the headquarters of Hawaii Volcanoes National Park, but finding the singer is a real challenge. The ‘Oma‘o is mainly a fruiteater, shown here eating bright red berries of native pilo. In any mountain forest on Hawai‘i one can expect to see the *‘io* or **Hawaiian Hawk**, which has two color phases. The dark one is mostly sooty black at all ages, while a lighter phase is brown above and white below as an adult, but has beautiful honey-colored juvenile plumage. The Big Island's honeycreeper specialties include the incredible **‘Akiapola‘au**, which you met previously on page 8, and the brilliant orange **‘Akepa**, smallest of the honeycreepers. ‘Akepas feed mainly among leaves where they search out insects, but they also sometimes sip nectar. The two parts of the ‘Akepa's finchlike bill are slightly crossed at the tip to aid in prying open places where insects can hide. The dull-plumaged **Hawai‘i Creeper** closely resembles the Hawai‘i ‘amakihi, but has a straighter bill and behaves more like a nuthatch, searching the bark of trees for insects. This native bird community is preserved in **Hakalau Forest National Wildlife Refuge**, the first such refuge to be established solely for forest birds. Even such protected areas cannot prevent the invasion of alien species such as the ubiquitous **Japanese White-eye**, shown here feeding on flowers of akala, the Hawaiian raspberry. A particularly insidious invader is the **Kalij Pheasant**, native to Himalayan forests and introduced as a game bird. The Kalij has become the vehicle of transport for seeds of a variety of noxious weeds and disease that are now showing up far from "civilization."

Hawaiian Hawk

Juvenile Hawk, light phase

'Akiapola'au

'Akepa

Hawai'i Creeper

Japanese White-eye

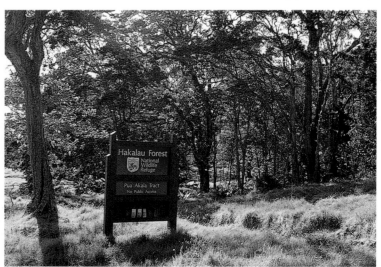

Kaliji Pheasant • DP

Hakalau Forest National Wildlife Refuge • DP

MAUI'S SPECIAL FOREST BIRDS

Maui also has its own set of specialties, all of which happen to be honeycreepers. For some reason, native solitaires and flycatchers either did not survive on Maui in historic times or never lived there at all. The island's most common endemic is the warbler-like **Maui 'Alauahio** or creepers, whose plumage resembles those of the Hawai'i 'Amakihi, but whose voice and behavior are quite distinct. Note the fairly straight bill on the grayish juvenile shown on the next page (a bright-yellow male is shown on page 7). The 'alauahio can be seen easily at Hosmer Grove in Haleakala National Park, which is also home to the "big three."

Maui's other two specialties have been found there as well, but to see them one usually has to venture far away from the highway. In **Waikamoi Preserve** (visitors are allowed here only by permit), a project of The Nature Conservancy adjacent to the national park, one can find both the spectacular **'Akohekohe**, also called Crested Honeycreeper, and sometimes the peculiar **Maui Parrotbill.** The 'akohekohe behaves somewhat like a giant 'apapane, feeding almost exclusively in ohi'a-lehua blossoms. Its odd gurgling song only enhances its rather bizarre plumage. Despite its superficially very dissimilar bill, the parrotbill's feeding methods are rather like those of the Big Island's 'Akiapola'au. It does not peck, but uses its lower mandible to gouge into fissures in the bark of trees, where it finds its main prey of beetle larvae. It may also crush small, dead twigs in its search and even opens pilo berries to look for grubs. Male Maui Parrotbills are brighter yellow and have bigger bills than females.

Maui 'Alauahio

'Akohekohe

Maui Parrotbill male

Maui Parrotbill female

Kalalau Valley • DP

A World Apart: The Kaua'i Forest

The distance between Kaua'i and O'ahu is the greatest separating any of the main Hawaiian Islands. This physical distance has had its effect on the evolution of Kaua'i's plants and animals. With a few exceptions, the entire community has a character all its own. It truly is a world apart. Although Kaua'i is smaller than Maui and Hawai'i, its mountain forests are much more accessible to the average visitor who can find many of its native birds around the overlooks above **Kalalau Valley**. Among them, the two red birds of the "big three" are what one expects, but in place of a single species of 'amakihi, Kaua'i has two that subdivide that niche. The **Kaua'i 'Amakihi** has a much longer and thicker bill than its relatives elsewhere and is much more

of a bark picker. Its companion species is the distinctive yellow **'Anianiau**, one of the smallest honeycreepers, with a straighter bill than 'amakihis and warbler-like habits. Also look for another little green bird sporting a yellow forehead and rump (visible as it flies away), blue-gray finchlike bill, and black face. This is the **'Akeke'e**, a close relative of the 'Akepa (see page 6). The 'Akeke'e also has crossed mandibles that it uses to wedge apart the scales of ohi'a leaf buds. Unlike its red-orange sister species which has broader tastes, the 'Akeke'e feeds almost exclusively in ohi'a trees. Much rarer than the three green birds is the bark-picking **'Akikiki**, formerly called Kaua'i Creeper, the most nuthatch-like of the honeycreepers. Shown here is a juvenile with

its bold white "spectacles." Adults have more dark feathering in the face. Along with the honeycreepers at Koke'e, look for the bold and friendly **Kaua'i 'Elepaio**. The young birds, which are rusty brown rather than gray on the head, are particularly curious. One Kaua'i specialty that you should not expect to see without considerable time and effort is the very rare and endangered **Puaiohi**. Like all Hawaiian solitaires, the **juvenile Puaiohi** is spotted below. A second solitaire, the larger but similar-looking Kama'o, survived in very low numbers on Kaua'i until recently, but apparently succumbed to killer Hurricane Iniki in 1992. None has been seen since. It is only the latest in a growing list of species to disappear from Kaua'i's mountain forests, which

Kaua'i 'Amakihi

'Akeke'e

'Akikiki

'Anianiau

Kaua'i 'Elepaio adult

Kaua'i 'Elepaio juvenile

still harbored all their historically known species as recently as 1970. A particularly tragic loss was the **Kaua'i 'O'o**, a magnificent vocalist and the last member of its family (the honey*eaters*, not to be confused with honey*creepers*) in Hawai'i. The 'o'o survived in the remote Alaka'i Wilderness into the 1970's, when Pratt took the photo shown here. By the early 1980's, it was reduced to a single pair, the female of which disappeared after Hurricane Iwa in 1983. The Kaua'i 'O'o has not been reported since 1987.

Puaiohi adult

Puaiohi juvenile

Kaua'i 'O'o • DP

49

Mamane forest at Pu'u La'au • DP

MAUNA KEA'S DRY FOREST

Palila

Not all of Hawai'i's native forests are rain forests. On the Big Island, a distinctive open dry forest high on the leeward slope of Mauna Kea harbors a unique community of native birds. The parklike forest is dominated by the yellow-flowered mamane tree, a member of the pea family. Mamane is the main food source of the endangered **Palila**, a finch-billed honeycreeper that is the crown jewel of the dry montane forest. With its golden-yellow head and breast, the palila blends in beautifully with the mamane blossoms. It feeds not on nectar, but on seeds. The bird plucks a green seed pod and, holding it against a branch with its feet, rips open a seam to get at the orange-yellow seeds. The mamane forest also supports populations of the "big three," but the **'Apapane**, and the **'I'iwi**, both of which are stunning among the yellow flowers, are mostly seasonal visitors that follow the blooming cycle. On the other hand, the third member of the trio, the **Hawai'i 'Amakihi**, reaches its greatest population density anywhere in the high mamane forest. Probably 90 percent of individual native birds in the forest are Hawai'i 'Amakihi! Sharing the forest with the honeycreepers is a subspecies of **Hawai'i 'Elepaio** that is restricted to this habitat. It is characterized by having much white feathering around the head and in being paler overall than 'elepaios that live in wet forests (see page 42). Often flying high over the entire community is the **Short-eared Owl**. For some reason, the Hawaiian Hawk is only a rare visitor here.

'Apapane

Palila

Hawai'i 'Amakihi

'I'iwi

Hawai'i 'Elepaio

Short-eared Owl

Alien Invaders Storm the Ramparts

Hawai'i's surviving native birds are by no means safe in their mountain retreats. The recent sudden loss of so many birds from the forests of Kaua'i shows how tenuous a hold the native organisms have on continued existence. Birds that used to ride out the storms-of-the-century such as Hurricane Iniki now cannot do so because valleys that once provided safe refuge are now pestilential death traps. The onslaught of alien organisms, from viruses to mammalian predators, continues to eat away at the islands' biological heritage. Disease-free areas become inexorably smaller and smaller, as mosquitoes adapt to higher and higher elevations. They are aided in their spread by **feral pigs**. The ancient Hawaiian kept their pigs like barnyard animals, but modern pigs have been "bred up" for improved hunting by release of huge European boars. Pigs plow through the forest undergrowth like animated bulldozers, destroying the native plant cover,

Feral Pig

Pig damage in forest (right of fence)

Roof Rat

Po'o-uli • DP

House Finch

DP

It is difficult to realize that the lovely grasslands of today's Hawaiian ranches were created mostly by introduced mammals. When Captain Vancouver presented Kamehameha I with turkeys, he also gave him cattle and goats. Turned loose in the forests, these grazers proved far more effective in converting forest to pasture than outright logging would ever have been. The particularly important mixed forests of koa and ohi'a were especially vulnerable, because saplings of the dominant trees have no defense against grazers. Shown at right is a sequence that demonstrates how the prevention of regeneration by grazing destroys a forest without a single tree being logged! As you drive up the slopes of Haleakala on Maui, where groves of exotic eucalyptus dot lush pastures, try to remember that the area was once a koa/ohi'a rain forest alive with native birds. The **House Finches** of today are a poor exchange for parrotbill, 'alauahio, and 'akohekohe.

DP

opening the ground for invading weeds, and leaving pools ideal for mosquito larvae. The contrast between a pig-damaged forest and a protected one can be striking. On Maui, a native bird called the **Po'o-uli** that was only discovered in 1973 has subsequently been nearly wiped out by pig damage to its understory habitat. (It has never been adequately photographed and is shown in a Pratt painting.) Another insidious threat in the rain forests is the **roof rat**, a far more serious predator than most people realize.

DP

Northwest slope, Haleakala, Maui • DP

Hawaiian Crow or 'Alala

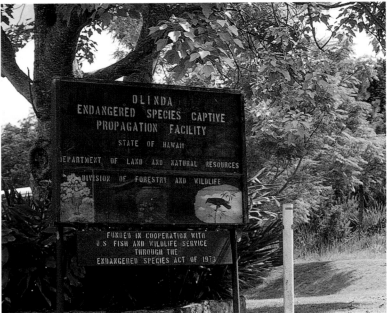

Olinda Endangered Species Facility Sign • DP

The Embattled 'Alala

Historically, Hawai'i was home to only a single member of the widespread crow family, the **Hawaiian Crow** or **'Alala**. Crows worldwide are often thought of as highly adaptable and nearly indestructible birds, but the plight of the Hawaiian species shows that even birds well equipped for survival can stand only so much abuse. Indeed, the 'alala is perhaps the quintessential illustration of what is wrong with Hawaiian ecosystems today. The crow originally had a rather enigmatic distribution, common in the forests of Kona, but absent from seemingly suitable habitats elsewhere on the Big Island. From subfossil remains, we now know that it is the sole survivor of several crow species that once lived throughout the Hawaiian Islands. The others disappeared after the Islands' habitats were altered by the first Polynesian settlers. A small captive flock at the Olinda Endangered Species Facility on Maui was highly inbred and consequently having disap-

pointing breeding success. Now, the McCandless Ranch in South Kona harbors the last three known wild breeding pairs, and heroic efforts are belatedly being made there to save Hawai'i's last crow from extinction.

Hawaiian crows are typical in being large, conspicuous, rambunctious birds that eat a wide variety of foods. They have a huge repertoire of wierd and wonderful vocalizations and, instead of the *caaw* of mainland crows, they utter a loud, high-pitched scream. Up to the 1960's, they remained fairly common around Kona ranches, but they were generally disliked and often shot as a nuisance. Their habit of following pig hunters through the forest and loudly announcing their presence certainly did not endear them to local people, but outright persecution alone cannot explain the bird's sudden decline in recent decades. Studies in the 1970's revealed a severe lack of breeding success. Some eggs and nestlings were taken by rats, and

others fledged only to mysteriously disappear. We now know that 'Alala fledglings, before they can fly, spend several days on the ground during which time they are vulnerable to mongooses and feral cats. Also, adult birds are often afflicted with avian malaria and bird pox, although these infections are not always fatal. Add to these threats the ongoing deforestation and other habitat changes, and the outlook for the 'Alala is indeed bleak.

Following years of bickering among various concerned parties, a new program managed by The Peregrine Fund holds some promise for saving the crow. Biologists remove eggs from wild nests and hatch them in incubators. Some incubator chicks join the captive birds at Olinda, but the rest are released to join the wild flock. Great care is taken to prevent the birds from becoming tame. Hatchlings are fed with crow hand puppets and, when handled, are fitted

Crow aviary • DP

'Alala with falconer's hood • DP

with falconer's hoods. Once they are old enough, the fledglings are "hacked" into an aviary in the rain forest of McCandless Ranch to acclimate them to the area and allow them to learn to eat natural foods. This period of captivity gets the young birds safely through their vulnerable terrestrial period. Before release, the birds are treated for pox lesions and malaria and fitted with radio transmitters so their movements can be traced. Wild pairs renest after removal of early clutches, but chicks hatched in the wild still have a very low survival rate. By 1994, the second year of the program, the wild population had increased for the first time in years and the captive birds produced the most chicks (at least four) in one season since 1981—results beyond anyone's wildest dreams. Since then, success has been less spectacular, but at least there is now hope that one of Hawai'i's rarest forest birds may live into the next century.

'Alala pair feeding in pilo tree

'Alala foot showing bird pox lesion • DP

HOME PORT FOR OCEAN WANDERERS

Visitors are often surprised that Hawai'i has no "seagulls." The reason is simple—gulls are scavengers of shallow continental shorelines in mostly temperate regions. In fact, the few gulls that do manage to make it to the islands never survive very well. Instead of gulls, Hawai'i is home to members of several families better adapted to feeding in deep, warm waters. Such birds include boobies, terns, tropicbirds, shearwaters, frigatebirds, and albatrosses.

Masked Booby • DP

Sooty Tern

Manana Island, Oahu • DP

Brown Noddy

Red-footed Booby

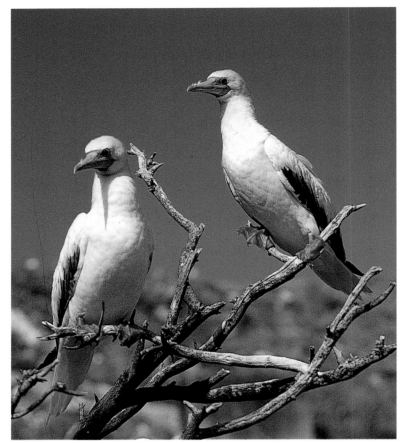
Red-footed Booby • DP

OUTWITTING THE PREDATORS

Seabirds generally require predator-free islands on which to nest. Ground-nesting birds such as the **Masked Booby** breed only on offshore islands such as Manana off Oʻahu, but can be seen flying over the adjacent shoreline. **Sooty Terns** nest in such numbers that from shore they look like a cloud of smoke over an island. At closer range, we can hear their raucous *wide-awake* cries. They sometimes fly inland at night, when their calls may seem a mockery to those trying to sleep. Among the Sooty Terns one can find the **Brown Noddy**, a tern with uncharacteristically dark feathering. Some seabirds avoid predators by nesting off the ground in trees (note that most mongooses are poor climbers, although a few have been observed climbing trees in Kipahulu Valley). The **Red-footed Booby** maintains colonies on both Kauaʻi and Oʻahu. They feed at sea mostly at night, so can be seen sitting in their colonies all day. The chicks begin life with a fluffy white down that is replaced by a dull gray-brown juvenile plumage by the time the bird fledges. Although the boobies have found ways to thwart ground predators, they still must contend with their old nemesis, the **Great Frigatebird**. These graceful scissor-tailed pirates harass incoming boobies to make them disgorge their catch of fish or squid. The frigatebird then catches it before it hits the water. In the breeding season, you might see a male frigatebird with his throat pouch inflated like a red balloon as a display to the female, identified by her white breast.

Red-footed Booby with chick • DP

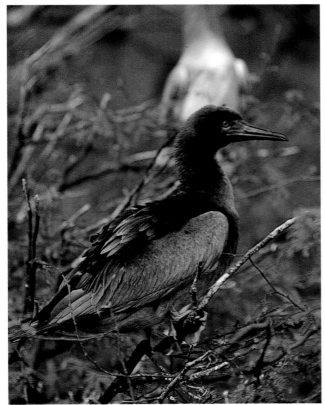

Red-footed Booby juvenile • DP

Great Frigatebird male • DP

Great Frigatebird female

Other seabirds have solved the predator problem by choosing nest sites on sheer cliffs. The ethereal **White-tailed Tropicbird** is widespread in the islands and even flies over rain forests far inland. It can be seen in such improbable places for a seabird as Kaua'i's Waimea Canyon and the caldera of Kilauea Volcano on the Big Island, where it nests on ledges despite the sulphurous fumes. Local people call them "crater birds." The **Red-tailed Tropicbird** is seen in only a few areas such as Kilauea Point on Kaua'i and Makapu'u on O'ahu, but at both places they put on a spectacular show with their somersaulting flight display involving three birds. Red-tailed tropicbirds nest only on seaward-facing cliffs. Another cliff nester is the **Black Noddy**. Look for it along Kaua'i's Na Pali Coast or the sea cliffs of Hawaii Volcanoes National Park. It is similar to the brown noddy but is smaller, darker, and has a contrasting gray tail as an adult.

White-tailed Tropicbird • DP

Red-tailed Tropicbird • DP

Black Noddy • DP

Kilauea Point National
Wildlife Refuge • DP

UNDERGROUND SEABIRDS

It is a surprise to many that some seabirds, such as shearwaters and petrels that spend most of their lives in exuberant flight over open seas, begin life in holes in the ground. That is indeed the case for one of Hawai'i's commonest seabirds, the **Wedge-tailed Shearwater**. If you go fishing offshore, you are sure to see these mouse-gray birds coursing low over the waves on stiffly held wings. They do indeed seem to shear the water with their wingtips. For nesting, wedge-tails choose offshore islets or the tips of promontories on the main islands that provide a degree of protection from predators. A typical site that is also a good place to observe their habits is **Kilauea Point National Wildlife Refuge** on Kaua'i. Although the parent birds come and go mostly at dawn and dusk, a few can be seen on the ground during midday. The fluffy gray chicks hunkered down in their cozy burrows are a delight. At night, the birds fill the air with eerie braying cries that might seem ghostly to the uninformed. **Newell's Shearwater** also nests in burrows, but these are in scattered localities high in the mountains, with most of the population on Kaua'i. When their chicks fledge in the fall, they leave their burrows at night and follow an innate drive to fly toward the brightest part of the sky (which used to be the distant horizon or the moon—in either case toward the sea, away from the island). Nowadays, however, the bright lights of towns and resorts confuse many birds, especially on cloudy nights, and the birds rain down on lawns and parking lots. Many are killed each year by cars, cats, and dogs. Shearwater feet are placed for swimming, and the birds cannot walk on, or take off from, level ground. They are not injured, but need a helping hand. If you find a grounded shearwater, take it to the nearest fire station, where it will be kept for safe release.

Wedge-tailed Shearwater

Wedge-tail chick in burrow • DP

Newell's Shearwater • DP

Laysan Albatross

RETURN OF THE ALBATROSS

The largest and in many ways most impressive of seabirds are the albatrosses. Until the past two decades, albatrosses have been long gone from the main Hawaiian Islands, although they continued to nest in large numbers on the uninhabited islands that stretch west to Kure Atoll. Then, a few pairs of **Laysan Albatross** began attempting to nest on Kaua'i and O'ahu, initially with little success because dogs always got their chicks. With help from man, however, a thriving colony has become established at Kilauea Point, where they put on one of the best wildlife shows in the islands. Courtship begins in December when pairs engage in their bowing and strutting display, accompanied by weird braying and whistling. Later, the dumpy gray-brown chicks provide a striking contrast to their sleek parents. Even the adults are not very graceful on the ground and often end their magnificent fixed-wing flights with a crash-landing. Such comical behavior earned them the nickname "gooney bird."

Laysan Albatrosses displaying

Laysan Albatross parent with chick